Everything
THAT Grows

Everything
THAT
Grows

Finding Your
Spiritual Rhythm
of Life *in* Christ

THOM GARDNER

Text design and typesetting by webbdezyne.com
Cover design by Karen Webb

ISBN: 978-1-500195-17-5

For Worldwide Distribution, Printed in the U.S.A.

1 2 3 4 5 6 / 17 16 15 14

Table of Contents

Introduction

Everything that grows, whether in the natural realm or in the spirit realm, follows the same repeated cycle—a continuum of growth that Jesus described in one of His metaphorical pictures of the kingdom of God. Here we define the kingdom of God as the ever-increasing influence of the life and peace of Christ in and through us.

Jesus compared this cycle of natural growth to the growth of his life in people. I have simply recognized and labeled four parts of the cycle of the *rhythm of growth* in the life of Christ. They are *resting*, *awakening*, *growing*, and *reproducing*.

"The kingdom of God is like a man who casts seed upon the soil (Resting); and he goes to bed

at night and gets up by day, and the seed sprouts and grows—how, he himself does not know. The soil produces crops by itself; first the blade (Awakening), then the head (Growing), then the mature grain in the head (Reproducing). But when the crop permits, he immediately puts in the sickle, because the harvest has come." (Mark 4:26–29 NASB)

In nature, seeds carry the DNA of a life form that is transplanted into the earth to reproduce more of the same life. Corn comes from corn, potatoes from potatoes, frogs from frogs. We don't get frogs from dogs. Jesus says that we recognize people or seeds by the fruit they produce. "You can identify them by their fruit, that is, by the way they act. Can you pick grapes from thorn bushes, or figs from thistles?" (Matthew 7:16 NLT) It is the same in spiritual growth. So we may identify this rhythm of the life of Christ in us in the same way: *Resting, awakening, growing,* and *reproducing.* These four movements are in turn associated with practices or *rhythms of the heart* that lead to growth in the life of Christ.

Further, this same rhythm provides a holistic and integrated pattern for prayer, marriage, discernment, and communication with God and people. For example, when we pray it is best to begin with a time of *quieting* focus where we tune out noise. Then have a time of *listening* to the heart of God and pray what we hear. As we pray, there is *growing* and healing as we allow God, by his Spirit, *reproducing* His heart and will in us.

Heart Cultivation

1. Consider the various rhythms or habits in your life. What kinds of rhythms do you find in your daily life?

2. Where are you growing in your personal life? In relationships with God and people? In character? In peace?

3. What have the three greatest changes been in the past 5 years of your personal life.

CHAPTER I

Heart Rhythms
of Resting

In the spiritual realm, resting refers to the life and peace of Christ resting in our hearts. In rest we focus on the seed of the Christ-life in times of silence—much as a seed rests quietly in the soil after it is planted. In order for a seed to be planted in the earth, a furrow must be created and the ground broken open to receive the seed. "Sow for yourselves righteousness; reap steadfast love; break up your fallow ground, for it is the time to seek the LORD, that he may come and rain righteousness upon you." (Hosea 10:12 ESV) In the spiritual growth, plowing is the act of confession that says we want to reproduce the life of Christ.

In the natural, when a seed is planted in the soil an aperture opens in the seed to receive moisture from the soil. In the spiritual, resting allows us to open ourselves up to be restfully available to the watering of the Spirit. Resting is mostly about quieting the inner and outer noise of our lives to focus on the person of Christ.

In order to grow, we need to rest as a seed rests in the soil after it is planted. The idea of resting is a wordless conversation with God where we simply allow ourselves to be enfolded in the loving presence of Christ. This is not just a mental exercise, but a mindful focus on the presence of Christ through personal worship in silence. Silence before God is an act of worship itself, a demonstration of utter trust in God. "But the LORD is in his holy temple; let all the earth keep silence before him." (Habakkuk 2:20 ESV) I am becoming His holy temple. I turn away from every other life to be present to the Christ in me.

Many times thoughts and concerns take up space in our heads and hearts and compete with the presence of God. These thoughts may have to do with ministry or finances or the kids. Jesus was great at rest and connecting with the heart of the Father during his earthly ministry. He modeled that value to his followers.

Resting renews us as we wait in the embrace of God. Resting positions us for connection with the Spirit of God. "I wait quietly before God, for my victory comes from him." (Psalms 62:1 NLT) In resting we are paying attention to the present moment in the presence of God. We are breathing in and filling our lungs with the breath of God. The same breath that created us out of the dust recreates us in the present moment.

Personal Daily Rhythm of Resting

Here are a few thoughts on incorporating the rhythm of rest into your daily living. Set aside a time during the day when you can sit in silence. This may be in your favorite chair in a living room or it may be in your car as you arrive at your place of work or a park by a stream in the woods. The place is not important; the focus is what is important. Be mindful of His breath in you. Quiet the inner noise of competing thoughts and preoccupations with life issues. Give those thoughts and concerns to Jesus to hold so that you can be open to Him. (Sometimes it helps to envision yourself handing those concerns to Jesus.) This is a time of intentional quiet and focus, not the downloading of new information. You may take anywhere from a few minutes to half an hour or longer. The length of time is not as important as your intention to be with Christ. You may do this several times each day.

You may use this resting time to focus on a word or phrase of Scripture you are reading. The idea of resting rhythms is not Bible study, or reading a book, though those are profitable for other heart rhythms. We might choose a phrase from Isaiah 26:3, "You will keep in perfect peace all who trust in you, all whose thoughts are fixed on you!" (Isaiah 26:3 NLT) Consider the phrase, "perfect peace." Speak it softly each time to exhale in your breathing. This focusing phrase is like a bookmark for the presence of God. Each time the inner or outer noise wants to take center stage in us during our time of resting, we simply return to the phrase or word and give it our attention.

Another resting practice can be visually reflecting on a scriptural narrative scene such as the apostles of Jesus returning to Him after a frenzy of ministry activity. "The apostles returned to Jesus from their ministry tour and told him all they had done and taught. Then Jesus said, "Let's go off by ourselves to a quiet place and rest awhile." He said this because there were so many people coming and going that Jesus and his apostles didn't even have time to eat. So they left by boat for a quiet place, where they could be alone.

(Mark 6:30–32 NLT) You may place yourself in the boat with those other intimate followers of Jesus and come to rest with Him.

Perhaps you can take time to join those beloved followers of Jesus for a time of rest. Get into the boat and leave the routine behind on the shoreline. Set sail for rest and reconnect with Jesus. Don't spend this time seeking a word from God—seek the God of the Word.

Seasonal Rhythms of Resting

Set apart regular times each week, month, quarter or year to go to a quiet place such as a retreat center or a place by water to soak in the presence of God. This can be a day or longer when you simply pay attention to your heart and gaze on the face of Christ. Though you may come away with some kind of revelation, your main purpose is to live and breathe in the presence of God in a quiet setting.

Marriage Rhythms of Resting

If you are married, set aside time on a regular basis to be alone with your spouse, to be quiet together in the presence of God. This can be as simple as a daily space together where you pray the scriptures over one another or take a walk together. You may choose a weekend getaway but not necessarily marriage conferences, though some conferences include times of quiet and rest. Remember that God created the Sabbath for man and not the other way around. The purpose of rest is quiet connection with God and each other. Marriages need space to rediscover the heart rhythms of resting in Christ together, to *awakening* to His voice. In resting together we grow and heal the bumps and bruises of real life. We establish communication and get back to the roots and come back to the table with nothing between our faces. Resting together resets and prepares our hearts to hear God together.

Community Rhythms

Leadership teams, small groups, or ministry teams should set apart a regular time retreat that includes times of silence each year. It is also a good idea that there be a few minutes of silent reflection at the beginning of any meeting or gathering so that those attending may be quiet in order to hear the Voice more clearly. Members of the community should engage one another as to the other's personal spiritual rhythm.

In communication with people, we should practice more quieting our hearts for the judgments and opinions regarding the person at the other end of our conversations. "Understand this, my dear brothers and sisters: You must all be quick to listen, slow to speak, and slow to get angry." (James 1:19 NLT)

As we grow in quieting and rest in God, the seed of Christ's life rests in the soil of our hearts, and we become focused on the present moment with Christ. As we are resting in Christ, the Holy Spirit waters that seed to release it's DNA to awaken new growth and conversion in us. This leads us to the Heart Rhythms of *Awakening*.

Heart Cultivation

1. How do you observe times of rest in your daily life?

2. Where are there moments in your daily living that you might establish short spaces for quieting your heart to listen to God?

3. What things tend to rob you of rest? Work? Worry? Busyness?

CHAPTER 2

Heart Rhythms
of Awakening

Once a seed has been planted and is resting in the soil, it eventually awakens in germination and sends a blade or sprout through the soil. This blade breaks through in order to connect to the sun, a higher life form in the process of photosynthesis. Before that the seed lived off of its own resources under the ground. But now it moves toward the higher source of life in the sun. Jesus said that in order for something to reproduce and grow, there would have to be a death. "I tell you the truth, unless a kernel of wheat is planted in the soil and dies, it remains alone. But its death will produce many new kernels—a plentiful harvest of new lives." (John

12:24 NLTSE) Until the seed awakens and pushes through to the sun, it lives off of its own resources. When awakening happens, it shifts to the higher source. In a spiritual sense, once the seed of the Christ-life has been planted in us it begins to move toward a higher source of life and peace. We cease striving and come to know God in deeper ways. (Psalm 46:10) This is like the spiritual process of conversion from our old life to the new in Christ. The life of Christ in me grows through the life and Spirit of the word of God. "It is the Spirit who gives life; the flesh profits nothing; the words that I have spoken to you are spirit and are life." (John 6:63 NASB) I am awakened to the life of Christ and stretching toward a new source of life beyond my own resources or what I have accomplished and what I know intellectually. I do this through hearing the voice of Christ, through meditation in the words of Christ through scripture, and through the human voices around me. "...grow in the grace and knowledge of our Lord and Savior Jesus Christ. To Him be the glory, both now and to the day of eternity." (2 Peter 3:18 NASB)

Personal Daily Formation

Our personal rhythm or awakening may include reflective reading in the Scriptures along with journaling insights and challenges from the word of God.

We in western Christianity tend to read for content and understanding. Reflective reading focuses on the presence of God in the word. When we read reflectively the Scriptures become the still refreshing waters to which we are led by the voice of the Shepherd Himself. It is good to establish a regular reading program but also a reflective reading program. We may read reflectively by choosing a short passage from the Scriptures and reading it three to four times slowly either aloud or silently. Read it the first time as if you were taking a bite of your favorite food. Read it a second time to chew on it a bit releasing the flavor noticing any words or phrases that stand out to you. Read it a third time prayerfully speaking the word back to the Lord with a grateful heart. Read it a fourth time to savor it. This is the "Mmmmmm" time where it goes deep to regenerate and revive us.

Personal Seasonal Formation

Take regular times to read through whole books of Scripture reflectively. Read visually seeing the beautiful narratives of Scripture come alive. Don't read to merely define words.

Community Formation

Meet for lunch or coffee on a regular basis with a friend or two. There are to be no discussions of ministry or business. These are times of listening to the heart of Jesus together. Engage in conversations across the table and hear the word of God that has been implanted in a friend's heart and life. Don't try to out do one another with clever revelations and thoughts. Or, you may wish to expand your reading group by choosing a passage to read with a small group. One can read the passage out loud slowly while the others reflect and share by praying the truths in the scripture over one another. We are inviting Christ to come into His temple—us—to overturn the tables of merchandise that His house would be a house of prayer not business.

We also must read to gain understanding of the mind of Christ. This requires deeper inductive study where we engage the Word of God thoughtfully. Reading Scripture can be reflective and also include rigorous study tools available.

Heart Cultivation

1. When do you live in your own natural abilities and forget to seek God for help and wisdom? These are places of our comfortable default.

2. Have you tried reading the Scriptures reflectively envisioning the biblical scene? Choose a favorite passage now and read with your spiritual eyes opened.

CHAPTER 3

Heart Rhythms of Growing

As I continue to grow toward the *source* of life, I become aware of things that may be obstacles to growth such as we would find in any garden; *rocks*, *roots*, and *sticks*. Unless we remove them they will become obstacles to further growth.

Rocks

Rocks are the hard places in my heart that cannot receive or reproduce the life of Christ. These are places where my heart has become hardened and closed to the will and voice of Heaven. They may be the result of disappointments. We may have formed expectations about how life and those

people close to us should respond to us. Many times the hard places come from our human expectations that compete with the purposes of God. When our expectations are not met, we form judgments that become hardened places resulting in disconnection with God or people. We are then no longer open.

Unmet   Hardened
Expectations / Judgements / Hearts / Separation

Rocks are places where my *wants* overcome God's *will*. These rocks may show up in our community life together as reactions from unsurrendered areas of my heart. Here are six indications in our behavior where hardened places in our hearts are not open to connection or correction by the Spirit of God or through the community of God's people. The seed of God's word tends to bounce off the hardened soil in our hearts.

Denial	versus	Acceptance
Defensiveness	versus	Vulnerability
Dismissiveness	versus	Valuing
Deflection	versus	Openness
Dislike	versus	Affection
Distrust	versus	Trust

Roots

Roots are those issues that live in our hearts that compete with the life of Christ like weeds in a garden. In order to identify these roots I must ask, "What is living between my face and the face of God?" (See author's book *Healing the Wounded Heart; Overcoming Obstacles to Intimacy With God*, Destiny Image Publishers.) The roots living in our hearts may be lies or beliefs that came into our hearts as a result of past wounding or cultural programming. Lies and false beliefs result in negative self-talk such as, "I'm alone", "I don't belong", "I'm not as good as...", "I'm not good enough", "I must be in control", "I'm dirty", or "There is no hope." These also identify areas of core needs we may try to fulfill on our own. Some have a need for value so they perform to gain attention. Some may need affirmation or security. We can identify these roots by emotions and resulting behaviors as we may overreact to a relatively minor situation. For example: One of your children spills milk on the diner table and you launch into a tirade against them? The anger is coming from somewhere off the table in the past. It's about more than spilled milk.

Roots compete with the life of Christ in us and take our attention from God and put it on ourselves. They are lies and distortions mostly about the heart and love of God. These roots are uprooted by going back to the places where lies became a part of us and uprooting them. An example of this would be when Peter denied Jesus three times by a charcoal fire (John 18:18). Jesus restored him three times by a charcoal fire (John 21:19). Jesus took Peter back to the scene of his denial at a charcoal fire in order to restore him and uproot the shame of his denial. Otherwise, Peter may have been lost and self-focused on shame for the rest of his life.

Sticks

Sticks are obstacles that used to be alive in me but are alive no longer. They are the remnants of last years crop that produce no fruit now. They may be traditions of religion that have faded from our memory and meaning. They may be habits or the way we are used to doing things that have not been looked at for awhile. We can determine what or where these sticks are by asking what kind of fruit they produce—whether they are life-giving or simply in the way of our spiritual growth.

Personal and Seasonal Formation

To uproot what is competing or getting in the way of Christ's life in us, we need to pay personal attention to our own heart's inner conversations. Again, the aspects of *resting* and *awakening* are important as we pay attention to what stands out to us. Where do we overreact? Where do we form judgments or hold unforgiveness? Many times reflective reading and meditation in the Scriptures will provide a contrast that reveals our hearts to us when the Word of God does not feel true to us personally. (A book you may find helpful as you continue to grow is the author's book, *The Healing Journey, An Interactive Guide to Spiritual Wholeness*, Destiny Image Publishers.)

Taking regular times to look at the *rocks, roots* and *sticks* together with a spiritual director or close friend will be helpful. Pray together with listening hearts to find places of past wounding or disappointments and the underlying expectations. As you pray ask the Holy Spirit to reveal truth to you about those expectations and hardened places. "Then Christ will make his home in your hearts as you trust in him. Your roots will grow down into God's love and keep you strong. And may you have the power to understand, as all God's people should, how wide, how long, how high, and how deep his love is. May you experience the love of Christ, though it is too great to understand fully. Then you will be made complete with all the fullness of life and power that comes from God."(Ephesians 3:17–19 NLT)

Community Formation

It is important for teams or small groups to be as open and vulnerable to one another as possible. This requires establishing healthy group guidelines in order to facilitate a safe and welcoming environment where honest discussions may take place. We share our observations within the group "speaking the truth in love." (Eph. 4:15 NIV) Teams should prioritize the presence of God in meetings before the business. Take time to read scripture together reflectively and pray blessing over one another.

Heart Cultivation

1. Consider the rumblings of self-talk that go on in your heart? What kinds of rocks, roots, and sticks might be coming to the surface?

2. Think of a few key life events that have shaped your life? What were they and how did they influence your direction in life?

CHAPTER 4

Heart Rhythms
of Reproducing

The goal of all heart rhythms is that the love and life of Christ become part of us, that we are becoming more like Him. This calls for transformation and reproducing the seed of Christ's life that was placed in us at the beginning of the journey. There is a difference between mere change and transformation. We may make changes to a house, for example, by adding something to it, but the house remains the same. Transformation leads to something totally new. We have torn down the old house and built something altogether new that looks like the heart of Christ. We are reproducing the seed of the character and peace of Christ. I

know what is growing in me by the fruit it is producing through me. The question is, "Is the life, peace and humility of Christ becoming more evident in me? Am I growing in the fruit of the Spirit that Paul described?" (See the next section for a helpful survey.)

Rhythms of Individual Formation

(Individual and community reflection) The question, "What am I becoming?" needs to be asked to and answered by believers and those who lead them. We need input from the community around us. The following surveys may be helpful reference points. We realize that in our spiritual journey of reproducing the life of Christ each of us will encounter landmarks and land mines. How would you gauge your growth in the character of Christ? Three months from now? A year from now? We have included a survey in the next section of this book to identify areas of spiritual growth. It is suggested that you review the *Spiritual Maturity Survey* on a quarterly or semiannual basis to see where you have grown. You might sit down with your spiritual director or friend and ask what they see in your life.

The main question of reproducing the life of Christ in us is, "What am I becoming?" We ask ourselves and one another, "What do I believe?" or "What do you think?" but seldom take time to ask, "What am I becoming?" The answer to this question reveals what is rooted and growing in our hearts. Through following our own rhythm of spiritual life and practice we are removing whatever stands between God's face and our own so that we may reflect the glory of Christ in a darkened world. "But we all, with unveiled face, beholding as in a mirror the glory of the Lord, are being transformed into the same image from glory to glory, just as from the Lord, the Spirit." (2 Corinthians 3:18 NASB) What veils our faces?

Heart Cultivation

1. What is your life reflecting to others in your spiritual community?

2. Are you becoming more like Christ in your attitude and the level of peace you live in?

CHAPTER 5

Principles of
the Heart Rhythm

In the previous pages there were several suggestions regarding our finding and following a heart rhythm in each of the areas of *resting, awakening, growing* and *reproducing* in the lives of Christ-followers. These are not the only rhythms or practices available to us. There are no end of practices to help us grow in the character and peace of Christ. The variety of heart rhythms are as plentiful as there are people. We all have different lives with different rhythms. The college student may have a different rhythm than a policeman. The construction worker may have a different experience and need than a physician. Nonetheless, there

are principles that can lead all of us regardless of where we are as to profession or stage of life. These heart rhythms will likely change through the seasons of life.

What is a heart rhythm or spiritual practice? A heart rhythm is a regular part of our spiritual journey that...

- Is an intentional act or practice that moves us along a path closer to God.

- Puts our focus on Christ rather than self.

- Leads to growth in the character and peace of Christ.

- May flow through anything that is from God, including creation, that reflects His heart and character.

- Leads to *resting, awakening, growing* and *reproducing* Christ in us.

- May engage any or all of the five senses.

- May be followed individually or with others, whether with one or many.

In the following section you will be invited to establish your own rhythm of spiritual life. The ancients called this a "rule of life." The rule consisted of prayer and reading Scripture individually and in small groups. In the next section of this book you will identify areas for spiritual growth and begin to create your own rhythms of spiritual growth.

PREVIEW OF THE
SPIRITUAL MATURITY SURVEY

The Spiritual Maturity Survey that follows is simple and taken from Scripture. Paul describes the heart conditions of those who are growing in Christ. This is not a test to pass or fail. It is a survey to help us find areas where we might grow in the character and peace of Christ.

The survey is based on the *Fruit of the Spirit* listed in Galatians 5.

"But the Holy Spirit produces this kind of fruit in our lives: love, joy, peace, patience, kindness, goodness, faithfulness, gentleness, and self-control. There is no law against these things!" (Galatians 5:22–23 NLT)

We may look at each of these "fruits" individually to see areas for growth. These fruits are also grouped into general areas of spiritual growth focusing on our relationship with God, people, and formation of our own character.

Love Joy Peace	Formation from God
Patience Kindness Goodness	Formation toward People
Faithfulness Gentleness Self-control	Formation of Self

As you complete the survey look at each of the "fruits" but also consider them in the grouping above, looking at areas where you might grow in the formational traits from God, toward other people and yourself. Keep these areas in mind as you develop your own *Heart Rhythms for Growth*.

Again, this is not a test; it is a survey to help you grow in the love, peace and character of Jesus Christ. As we grow in these we are seeing the kingdom of God, the ever-increasing influence of the heart and character of Jesus Christ in us and through us to the world.

Blessings and peace to God's beloved: You!

Spiritual Maturity Survey

Directions for
Survey Completion

- Rate each of the following formational character traits from 1 to 5, 1 being the weakest and 5 the strongest.

- Total where indicated at the end of each group of three traits. The total for each group of three formational traits could range from 3 to 15. Any total under 8 should be considered an area for growth. (Consider adding scriptures for reflective reading in any of the areas identified as needing growth. You may also want to sit with a trusted friend or growth group to discuss the areas you have identified.)

- Note overall strength or weakness in Growth Upward Toward God, Growth Outward Toward Others, or Growth Inward Toward Transformation.

Growth Upward
Toward God

1   2   3   4   5

Love

Self-centered	o	o	o	o	o	Others-centered
Withholding	o	o	o	o	o	Generous
Uncaring	o	o	o	o	o	Caring

Total _____

Joy

Dissatisfied	o	o	o	o	o	Satisfied
Gloomy	o	o	o	o	o	Glad
Defeated	o	o	o	o	o	Triumphant

Total _____

Peace

Restless	o	o	o	o	o	At Rest
Insecure	o	o	o	o	o	Secure
Unsure	o	o	o	o	o	Confident

Total _____

Growth Outward Toward Other People

          1 2 3 4 5

Patience

	1	2	3	4	5	
Impatient	o	o	o	o	o	Patient
Reactive	o	o	o	o	o	Steady
Intolerant	o	o	o	o	o	Tolerant
						Total _____

Kindness

	1	2	3	4	5	
Unkind	o	o	o	o	o	Kind
Harsh	o	o	o	o	o	Mild
Inconsiderate	o	o	o	o	o	Considerate
						Total _____

Goodness

	1	2	3	4	5	
Unethical	o	o	o	o	o	Ethical
Uncharitable	o	o	o	o	o	Charitable
Ungodly	o	o	o	o	o	Godly
						Total _____

Growth Inward
Toward Transformation

	1	2	3	4	5	
Faithfulness						
Fearful	o	o	o	o	o	Trusting
Unreliable	o	o	o	o	o	Reliable
Dishonest	o	o	o	o	o	Honest
						Total _____
Gentleness						
Insensitive	o	o	o	o	o	Gentle
Non receptive	o	o	o	o	o	Teachable
Proud	o	o	o	o	o	Humble
						Total _____
Self-control						
Undisciplined	o	o	o	o	o	Disciplined
Volatile	o	o	o	o	o	Calm
Bound	o	o	o	o	o	Free
						Total _____

Create Your Personal Rhythm of Spiritual Life

What You Practice
On a Daily or Weekly Basis

Resting

Awakening

Growing

Reproducing

Seasonal Rhythms

*Everything* THAT Grows

What You Practice Monthly, Quarterly, Annually

Resting

Awakening

Growing

Reproducing

Community Rhythms
of
Spiritual Life

What You Practice
With Other Friends

Resting

Awakening

Growing

Reproducing

About the Ministry

Restored Life Ministries, Inc., is a ministry of accompanying and encouraging believers in their pursuit of the character and peace of Jesus Christ through spiritual growth. Our ministry is one of integrated spiritual formation including heart rhythms of inner *quieting* to enable *listening* to the voice of God resulting in *restoring* hearts on their journey of *becoming* like Him. These movements toward Christ happen through seminars, classes, individual formational sessions, retreats, and the production of written materials. For more details, or to invite one of our facilitators, refer to our ministry link. http://www.restoredlifeministries. com/index.html

Other Resources

Healing the Wounded Heart:
Removing Obstacles to Intimacy with God

http://www.alibris.com/Healing-the-Wound-
ed-Heart-Removing-Obstacles-to-Intimacy-
with-God-Thom-Gardner/book/9229991?-
matches=5

The Healing Journey:
An Interactive Guide to Spiritual Wholeness.

http://www.alibris.com/The-Healing-Jour-
ney-An-Interactive-Guide-to-Spiritual-Whole-
ness-Thom-Gardner/book/12119517?-
matches=19

Relentless Love:
Unfolding God's Passion, Presence, and Glory

http://www.alibris.com/Living-the-God-
Breathed-Life-An-Invitation-to-Rest-at-the-
Table-Thom-Gardner/book/15731220?-
matches=16